Sovereign Principles: Embodiment in Practice

A J Moore
Sovereign Frequency

Sovereign Principles

Paperback ISBN: **978-1-972967-04-1**

eBook ISBN: **978-1-972967-05-8**

Dedication

To those who realize that they are still here.

Sovereign Principles

How to Use This Book

This is not a book to be consumed once.

It is a framework to return to.

You can read it from beginning to end, or you can open it to the principle that meets your current position.

Each principle is designed for real-time application, not reflection alone.

Do not rush through it.

Apply it.

Return to it.

Let it meet you where you are.

Table of Contents

Sovereign Principles

Introduction

There comes a point where information is no longer the problem.

You've read enough.
You've heard enough.
You've considered enough perspectives to understand that more knowledge does not automatically create change.

The gap is not awareness.

The gap is embodiment.

Sovereign Principles exist to close that gap.

This is not a philosophy to admire.
This is not a system to memorize.
This is a framework to live.

Each principle represents a stabilized truth — not something to chase, but something to return to.
They are not rules imposed from the outside.
They are anchors that reveal what is already present when distortion is removed.

At the foundation of this system is a simple understanding:

Clarity does not come from adding more.
It comes from removing what does not belong.

When fear is removed, truth becomes visible.
When urgency is removed, direction becomes obvious.
When distortion is removed, execution becomes natural.

This is where Sovereign Principles operate.

Not in theory.
Not in performance.
But in real-time decision making.

These principles are designed to be revisited, not completed.

They will meet you differently depending on where you stand,
because you are not static.

Growth is not becoming something new.
It is recognizing what has always been there, and choosing to stand
in it consistently.

This is embodiment.

This is practice.

This is sovereignty.

Principle 0 — The Source

Nothing Sovereign originates from fear.
Fear produces reaction. Sovereignty requires intention.

Translation

Every action begins from a source.
That source determines the outcome before the action is even taken.
Fear does not create clarity. It creates urgency, pressure, and distortion.
When fear is present, the mind narrows. Options disappear. Timing feels immediate.
The objective shifts from accuracy to relief. This is reaction.
Sovereignty cannot be built on reaction. It requires intention, chosen, steady, and clear.
If the source is unstable, the result will be unstable.

Distortion

When fear becomes the source:
Decisions are rushed.
Control replaces awareness.
Outcomes are forced.
Energy is drained unnecessarily.

Application

Before any meaningful action, pause.
Ask, "Is this coming from fear, or clarity?"
If fear is present, do not act immediately.
Allow the signal to settle.

Anchor

If fear is leading, I am not.

Principle 1 — Authorship

Life does not just happen. It is authored through Sovereign practice.

Sovereign practice consists of foundational boundaries that maintain internal coherence.

Translation

Life will present events, conditions, and circumstances.

But the experience of life is not determined by what happens.

It is determined by how you interpret, how you respond, and what you reinforce over time.

Authorship means you are not drifting, reacting, or waiting for outcomes.

You are participating consciously in the direction of your life.

This does not mean control over everything.

It means responsibility for your choices within everything.

Distortion

When authorship is abandoned:

- Life feels random

- Responsibility is externalized

- Patterns repeat without awareness

- Blame replaces adjustment

It sounds like:

- "This always happens to me"

- "I had no choice"

- "That's just how things are"

Without authorship, life becomes something you endure instead of something you shape.

Sovereign Principles

Application

At any moment, you can reclaim authorship.

Not by controlling the situation, but by choosing your position within it.

Ask:

What am I creating right now through my response?

Then adjust:

- Choose clarity over reaction

- Choose direction over drift

- Choose responsibility over explanation

Small corrections restore authorship immediately.

Anchor

I am not at the mercy of my life. I am participating in its creation.

Principle 2 — Clarity

Nothing can be decided from a corrupted field.

Clarity must precede action.

Translation

Before any decision, there is a field.

That field is made up of thoughts, emotions, assumptions, and environmental pressure.

If the field is distorted, the decision will be distorted.

No amount of effort can correct a decision that was made from confusion.

Clarity is not something you add after the fact.

It is the condition required before action.

Without clarity:

- perception narrows

- meaning becomes unstable

- timing becomes reactive

With clarity:

- options become visible

- decisions become precise

- execution becomes efficient

Distortion

A corrupted field looks like:

- Emotional overload

- Urgency without understanding

- Conflicting thoughts

- External pressure influencing internal decisions

It sounds like:

- "I just need to decide something"

- "I don't have time to think about this"

- "Let me just move and fix it later"

This creates unnecessary mistakes, repeated corrections, and wasted energy.

Most people try to act their way into clarity. That never works.

Application

Before making a decision, check the field.

Ask:

Am I clear… or am I reacting?

If clarity is not present:

- Do not decide

- Do not force resolution

- Remove pressure where possible

- Allow the system to settle

Clarity returns when emotional intensity lowers, mental noise quiets, and perception widens.

Then decide.

Anchor

If the field is unclear, the answer is wait.

Principle 3 — Meaning

Meaning creates distortion. You create meaning.

Meaning must be consciously chosen.

Translation

Events do not carry inherent meaning. They happen.

Meaning is assigned after the event through interpretation.

That interpretation is influenced by:

- past experiences

- emotional state

- expectations

- beliefs

Without awareness, meaning is assigned automatically.

And automatic meaning is often inaccurate.

Once meaning is assigned, it shapes perception, emotional response, and decision-making.

This is how distortion forms.

Not from the event, but from the meaning attached to it.

Distortion

Unconscious meaning sounds like:

- "This means something is wrong"

- "They did that on purpose"

- "This always happens to me"

- "This is a problem"

These meanings feel real, but they are interpretations, not facts.

Once accepted, they create:

- unnecessary emotional weight

- misaligned decisions

- reactions based on assumption

Most people do not respond to reality.

They respond to the meaning they created about reality.

Sovereign Principles

Application

Separate the event from the meaning.

Ask:

What actually happened… and what am I making it mean?

Then choose intentionally:

- Remove unnecessary interpretation

- Avoid assigning motive without clarity

- Allow multiple possibilities

- Default to neutral until clarity is established

Meaning should support clarity, not replace it.

Anchor

The event is real. The meaning is mine.

Principle 4 — System Integrity

Normalizing distortion and dysfunction normalizes friction and leaks energy.

Translation

A system does not break all at once.

It breaks through what is tolerated.

Small distortions, when accepted repeatedly, become normalized.

What was once recognized as misalignment, inefficiency, or dysfunction begins to feel normal.

Once normalized, it is no longer corrected.

And what is not corrected compounds.

This creates friction.

Friction creates resistance, fatigue, and inefficiency.

Over time, energy begins to leak from the system.

Integrity is not maintained through intensity.

It is maintained through consistency in what is allowed and what is corrected.

Distortion

Loss of system integrity looks like:

- It's not a big deal

- I'll fix it later

- This is just how it is

- It's easier to leave it alone

These are not decisions. They are permissions for misalignment to remain.

Over time, this leads to:

- lowered standards

- reduced clarity

- increased effort for smaller results

The system begins to require more energy while producing less outcome.

Sovereign Principles

Application

Protect the system by correcting early.

Not aggressively, but consistently.

Ask:

Am I allowing something that I know is misaligned?

If yes:

- address it while it is small

- restore alignment immediately

- do not normalize it

This applies to behavior, environment, relationships, and internal patterns.

Integrity is maintained through small, accurate corrections over time.

Anchor

What I allow, I reinforce.

Principle 5 — Reset

Safety is the baseline for every reset.

Translation

Misalignment will happen.

No system remains perfect at all times.

The difference is not whether disruption occurs…

It is how quickly and accurately you return.

Reset is not avoidance, suppression, or escape.

Reset is intentional realignment.

But realignment cannot occur in a state of threat.

When the system feels unsafe:

- the body braces

- the mind narrows

- perception distorts

In that state, correction is not possible.

Safety restores openness, awareness, and regulation.

And only from that state can clarity return.

Distortion

When safety is ignored:

- resets are rushed

- emotions are suppressed

- action is forced prematurely

It sounds like:

- "I need to fix this now"

- "Let me just move past it"

- "I don't have time to deal with this"

This creates:

- incomplete resets

- repeated patterns

- deeper misalignment

Without safety, the system does not reset… it fragments.

Sovereign Principles

Application

When disruption occurs, do not immediately act.

First, restore safety.

This may look like:

- pausing

- stepping away

- breathing

- reducing external pressure

Ask:

Am I in a state where I can see clearly?

If not:

- do not decide

- do not correct yet

- allow the system to stabilize

Once safety is present:

- clarity returns

- perception widens

- correction becomes accurate

Then reset.

Anchor

No safety, no reset.

Principle 6 — Boundaries

Boundaries may evolve with the environment. They must never be compromised.

Translation

Boundaries define what is allowed, accepted, and engaged.

They are not rigid walls.

They are standards that preserve internal coherence.

As environments change, boundaries may adjust.

But the function of boundaries never changes:

to protect alignment.

Without boundaries:

- external influence overrides internal clarity

- pressure replaces intention

- misalignment enters the system repeatedly

Boundaries are not about control of others.

They are about clarity of self.

Distortion

Compromised boundaries sound like:

- It's not worth the conflict

- I'll just let it go this time

- I don't want to make this a thing

- They didn't mean it like that

These are not acts of understanding.

They are decisions to override internal clarity.

Over time, this leads to:

- resentment

- confusion

- repeated misalignment

- loss of self-trust

When boundaries are compromised, the system becomes unstable.

Sovereign Principles

Application

Establish boundaries from clarity, not emotion.

Ask:

What maintains my alignment in this situation?

Then:

- communicate it clearly when needed

- act in accordance with it consistently

- do not negotiate against your own clarity

Boundaries do not require force, explanation, or validation.

They require consistency.

When upheld:

- interactions become cleaner

- decisions become easier

- energy is preserved

Anchor

I do not negotiate against my own clarity.

Principle 7 — Abundance

Your gain does not require another's lack.

Translation

Most systems operate from scarcity.

They assume:

- resources are limited

- success is competitive

- one person's gain requires another's loss

This creates:

- comparison

- tension

- unnecessary conflict

Abundance operates differently.

It recognizes:

Value can be created, expanded, and shared.

Your progress does not diminish another's.

And another's success does not reduce your potential.

When scarcity is removed:

- focus returns to creation

- energy is preserved

- collaboration becomes possible

Distortion

Scarcity-based thinking sounds like:

- There's not enough

- If they win, I lose

- I need to get there first

- I can't share this

This creates:

- competition without purpose

- guarded behavior

- limited thinking

- unnecessary stress

Scarcity does not increase success.

It restricts it.

Sovereign Principles

Application

Shift from competition to creation.

Ask:

What can I create or expand here?

Instead of:

- comparing progress

- reacting to others

- protecting position

Focus on:

- increasing value

- refining your work

- building without dependency on others' outcomes

Abundance is not passive.

It is active creation without conflict.

Anchor

There is more when I create, not when I compete.

Principle 8 — Leadership

Power is not measured by what you conquer. It is measured by who you uplift.

Translation

Leadership is not dominance.

It is not control, force, or position.

True power is not demonstrated by:

- what you take

- what you win

- or what you control

It is demonstrated by what grows because of your presence.

Leadership is expressed through:

- clarity in action

- consistency in behavior

- alignment in decision-making

Others do not follow force.

They respond to stability, direction, and integrity.

Leadership is not something you claim.

It is something that becomes evident.

Distortion

Misaligned leadership looks like:

- control disguised as guidance

- authority without alignment

- influence driven by ego

- correction without understanding

It sounds like:

- Do it this way because I said so

- I know what's best

- They need to listen

This creates:

- resistance

- dependency

- disconnection

When leadership is forced, it weakens both the leader and the system.

Sovereign Principles

Application

Lead through alignment, not control.

Ask:

What does my presence create in this situation?

Then:

- act with clarity

- communicate without force

- allow others to choose

- support without overreaching

Leadership does not require validation, recognition, or compliance.

It requires consistency in alignment.

When practiced:

- others stabilize

- environments improve

- outcomes elevate naturally

Anchor

My power is reflected in what grows around me.

Principle 9 — Autonomy

Love and happiness are autonomous states. No one can give them to you.

Translation

Most people experience love and happiness as something received, dependent on others, or

something that can be gained or lost.

This creates dependency.

When external conditions change:

- emotional state changes

- stability is lost

Autonomy recognizes:

Love and happiness originate internally.

They are not created by others.

They are expressed through you.

Others can reflect, enhance, or share these states, but they do not create them.

When autonomy is established:

- emotional stability increases

- relationships become cleaner

- dependency is removed

Distortion

Emotional dependency sounds like:

- They make me happy

- I need this to feel okay

- If this changes, I'll lose everything

- I can't be without this

This creates:

- attachment without clarity

- fear of loss

- control-based behavior

- emotional instability

When happiness is externalized, control replaces connection.

Sovereign Principles

Application

Return emotional responsibility to self.

Ask:

Am I sourcing this feeling internally… or assigning it externally?

Then:

- stabilize your internal state first

- engage others from completeness, not need

- remove pressure from relationships

- allow connection without dependency

Autonomy does not remove connection. It purifies it.

Anchor

I bring the state. I do not search for it.

Principle 10 — Continuity

The path forward ensures a future.

Translation

Progress is not created through intensity.

It is created through consistent, aligned movement over time.

Many systems fail not because they are wrong,

but because they are unsustainable, inconsistent, or dependent on bursts of effort.

Continuity focuses on:

- what can be maintained

- what can be repeated

- what can be built upon

The goal is not rapid movement.

The goal is stable direction.

When the path is consistent:

- outcomes compound

- clarity strengthens

- effort becomes efficient

Distortion

Lack of continuity looks like:

- bursts of motivation followed by inactivity

- constant restarting

- shifting direction without completion

- dependence on intensity

It sounds like:

- I'll go all in today

- I need to catch up

- Let me push hard and fix everything

This creates:

- inconsistency

- fatigue

- incomplete systems

Without continuity, progress resets instead of building.

Sovereign Principles

Application

Choose the path you can sustain.

Ask:

Can this be maintained consistently?

Then:

- reduce unnecessary intensity

- focus on repeatable actions

- build momentum through consistency

- allow progress to compound

Continuity is not fast.

It is reliable.

And reliability creates long-term outcomes.

Anchor

Consistency creates what intensity cannot.

Principle 11 — The Sovereign Creed

Be yourself, at your very best, at all times.
Return to alignment.

Translation

All principles converge here.

The Sovereign Creed is not a statement of identity.
It is a standard of behavior.

Being yourself does not mean acting without awareness or
expressing every impulse.
It means operating in alignment with your highest level of clarity.

At your very best is not perfection.
It is awareness in action, intention in behavior, and consistency in
alignment.

At all times does not imply constant performance.
It implies consistent return.

You will drift.
You will encounter distortion.
You will experience misalignment.

The Creed is the mechanism of return.

Not through correction of the past, but through alignment in the
present.

Distortion

Misunderstanding the Creed sounds like:

"This is just who I am."
"I can't always be at my best."
"I'll fix it later."

These statements remove responsibility from the present moment.

They justify misalignment instead of correcting it.

Another distortion is performance:

Trying to appear at your best without being aligned internally.

This creates tension, inconsistency, and eventual collapse.

The Creed is not performance.
It is internal alignment expressed externally.

Sovereign Principles

Application

At any moment, return to the Creed.

Ask:
👉 *"Is this me, at my very best?"*

If yes:
Continue.

If no:
Adjust.

Not dramatically.
Not emotionally.
Just accurately.

Return to clarity.
Return to intention.
Return to alignment.

No delay.
No guilt.
No over-correction.

Just return.

Anchor

I return to alignment, again and again.

Sovereign Principles

Closing

Return to clarity.
Return to authorship.
Return to yourself.

Not once.
Not when it's convenient.
But as a practice.

You will drift.
You will encounter distortion.
You will move out of alignment.

Return anyway.

The work is not in learning more.
The work is in living what is already known.

Not perfectly.
But consistently.

Stand in it.
Return to it.
Live it.

About the Author

A J Moore is the creator of the Sovereign Frequency system, a practical framework focused on clarity, emotional mastery, and self-authored living.

His work emphasizes consistent alignment, real-time application, and the development of internal stability through structured principles rather than abstract theory.